P9-DXN-300

THE ART
OF
AQUATINT

THE THAMES AT TWICKENHAM by *Sir Frank Short*.

(*Courtesy of The New York Public Library*)

The Art of

AQUATINT

By B. F. MORROW

G·P· PUTNAM'S SONS

Publishers · NEW YORK · 1935

Copyright, 1935, by B. F. Morrow

A
MINTON BALCH
BOOK

Printed in the U. S. A.
VAN REES PRESS
New York

Foreword

IT is an undeniable fact that public interest in all forms
of print making is rapidly growing. Whatever be the
cause of this—whether it be the demand for smaller and
less expensive pictures to decorate the homes of today;
or that prints, being susceptible of multiplication, may be
more widely distributed and are therefore more readily
obtainable; or that more and more artists are turning to
this fluent and beautiful means of self-expression; or that
at last judicious and patient guidance on the part of
writers on and dealers in fine prints is beginning to bear
fruit—the fact remains, and is an ever-increasing source of
satisfaction to all those concerned with this great branch of
art. The power of the print to make mankind beauty con-
scious is a far-reaching one, and the power of such con-
sciousness in the advance of civilization is too vast to be
measured in words.

To dwell on the pleasure and profit, both emotional and
intellectual, to be derived from the study and appreciation
of fine prints would lead to pages where paragraphs are
desired. One thing cannot, however, be too strongly em-
phasized: no study can be wholly satisfactory nor can any
appreciation be complete without a fair understanding of
the technical processes that govern the principal print

media. The particular qualities characteristic of an etching, drypoint, line engraving, woodcut, wood engraving, aquatint, mezzotint, lithograph, or color print, must be understood by him who will enjoy to the utmost the message conveyed by one of these, and a knowledge of how such qualities were obtained by the artist is essential before the full recognition of them is possible.

There is still, in the public mind, a great uncertainty as to how, technically speaking, an etching is made, or an aquatint, or a lithograph, et cetera; and there is still, unfortunately, even among print makers, too great carelessness in the use of the terminology applicable to different processes. Histories are many: treatises which seek to describe such processes clearly and conscientiously, and in words easily grasped by all, are too few. There are, to be sure, numerous works which deal exhaustively with one or a few media, and a few which treat of all, but they tend to the highly technical and all too often are confusing to the layman or student. A beginning must be made and it is better to do so in brief and simple language and with stress upon fundamentals. More extensive and detailed familiarity will come with further study and by consulting those books which develop further the technical aspects of print making.

In the present work Dr. Morrow has described the making of an aquatint in such a way as to provide any one who may be interested in this fascinating and expressive medium with knowledge sufficient to enable him to recognize how an example under consideration was produced, and therefore to permit him the better to appreciate its merits. There are also hints bound to prove useful to any but the most experienced practitioner and even such a one must always be attentive to anything which may lead him to further discoveries. The field of aquatint has been widely explored and highly developed by many artists, and the sum total of writings on the subject is considerable, yet any such attempt as the present author has made to condense and simplify the matter for the benefit of those interested in the medium, yet unfamiliar with its technique, is a highly commendable one and should be given widespread support.

JOHN TAYLOR ARMS, N.A., S.A.E., A.R.E.

Table of Contents

List of Illustrations

xi

List of Illustrations

Introduction

As a result of articles written for that colorful periodical, *Prints,* on the subject of aquatint, I have received numerous requests for information and advice on this interesting medium of self-expression. The subject being too vast to incorporate in a perfunctory answer, I have finally submitted to these many requests (which in reality comprise the reason for my writing this decidedly modest book). For, surely, were there any textbook that adequately and simply described the various processes of aquatint, I would do no more than recommend it.

It is quite surprising that no such adequate presentation has been made on this subject since its introduction into England by Paul Sandby, as far back as 1775, discounting the salt and sulphur methods in slight use before that time. I attribute this lack of literature to the fact that the medium was used only for the production of tone in support of line. Also, as a medium that could stand alone as a distinct branch of the fine arts, aquatint was crowded out by the prevailing use of mezzotint and stipple engraving and the subsequent advent of lithography. Perhaps, too, the experimenting artists were unduly reticent about recording their valuable findings.

Hopefully, therefore, I offer this book to that lovable

character, the Artist, not as a completed science—for that would be impossible—but as guide for the development of this fascinating medium into ramifications yet to be disclosed by his individual ingenuity and imagination.

Many thanks to Frank A. Nankivell for much I have learned about aquatint, and for his enthusiastic assistance in making this treatise possible. In fact, it was with great difficulty that I managed to keep the name of this great aquatinter from appearing often enough to disclose my personal prejudice, and in the few instances where it does appear it was positively unavoidable. Many thanks also to the various artists whose works are herein reproduced for supplying me with the technical data of their respective masterpieces. I am also grateful for the moral encouragement given me by Frank Weitenkampf, that great authority and curator of prints at the New York Public Library, and for his eagerness in making me take this work seriously.

B. F. Morrow.

THE ART
OF
AQUATINT

Chapter I

REASONS FOR USE

BECAUSE this book is devoted primarily to aquatint, it will be taken for granted throughout the treatise that the art-student—or student-artist—is already familiar with all other branches of the etching art, particularly that of softground etching. This is so essential that the author advises the student to postpone the study of aquatint until such knowledge is acquired.

That advice may sound a bit dogmatic, but one must bear in mind that aquatint is not usually employed alone *but in combination with line*, the latter being used as a basis of procedure, either as guide for the stopping-out process or for strong definition and "bolster" work. No other line so effectively blends with the grain of aquatint as that produced by softground etching, though this may possibly be challenged by a delicately drawn roulette line.

However, there are many fine examples of pure aquatint, some of which embody a tremendous amount of detail and variation—as in night scenes of city streets—which make one marvel at the patience exercised by the

I

artist in alternately stopping-out, biting, and probably re-aquatinting. In such highly technical performances one would think it were easier to etch the subject entirely in line, but if the effect produced is the one the artist desired and strove for, then the extra time expended on aquatint has not been in vain.

It is true that there are numerous masterpieces which have been done in line with remarkable spontaneity and minimum of effort, and which effectively suggest mass, texture, et cetera, but many other line etchings could have told their respective stories far more successfully with mass biting.

It all comes down to a question of the quality of atmosphere or texture that is desired. A closely cross-hatched bitten area has a different quality, when printed, from a closely cross-hatched drypoint. Equally different in texture from these is an area deeply bitten in aquatint. To use one, instead of another, and *then* attempt to relieve one's conscience by saying, "Just as good," belies the artist's sincerity and belittles his artistic expression.

Let us assume, for example, that the artist reproduces his original sketch in each of three media—drypoint, etching and aquatint—being careful, of course, to retain the sketch's original values in each of these three kinds of engraving. The resulting prints, placed side by side, will

PLATE I.

TREEFORM by *Frank A. Nankivell.*

Original size, 11⅞ x 7⅛. Etching and Aquatint.

(Courtesy of Leonard Clayton Gallery)

show startling differences in atmosphere and texture (even though each could stand alone as a fine work of art). Which one of these will the artist designate as representing the true state of his artistic feeling? This problem is clearly demonstrated by the works of Goya, who often etched in line, was unsatisfied and added aquatint.

The value of aquatint for the purpose of color printing was early recognized by the old sporting-print makers. The minute receptacles etched by the acid into the copper are ideal for holding the applied color pigment. The aquatint base was found to give richer tones than that of stipple or line engraving, and is certainly more rapid and smooth in its application.

The most frequent use of aquatint, and more or less subservient to it, is probably in support of line. It is employed either over successive parts of the plate, for the production of tones and textures and for the separation of masses, or over the entire plate by a single biting for the purpose of "tying" objects together—as was so frequently done by Goya.

For the accentuation of the "note" in a composition, aquatint may be applicable in one of two ways: either by toning only the object itself, making it more or less dark in contrast with the rest of the plate, or by aquatinting everything on the plate except the note. This last usually

4

PLATE 2.

EPIC OF THE AIR by *Burnell Poole*.

Original size, 11⅜ x 16. Pure aquatint except for airplane; fine grain for distance, coarser grain for foreground (Chapter XIII.). *(Courtesy of* PRINTS)

calls for a skillfully applied graded biting—which will be described later—so that the eye goes easily and directly towards the "point of the story," which stands out in white relief.

Of course the most interesting use of aquatint is as a distinct medium, that is, by itself. Aquatint develops into a habit, and those who become addicted to it no longer think in terms of line, but in mass—any kind of mass— light or dark, thick or thin, definite or amorphous. The man who uses aquatint doesn't merely *suggest* tone, tex- ture, color, he actually *denotes* them. He doesn't merely outline, but paints with brush and varnish and mordants. He is no longer content with simple flat planes, but now models—as in any plastic medium—and achieves form, depth and perspective.

But—ah, there's the rub—the technique must be ren- dered subservient to the master's artistic genius; time and labor must be added to patience; difficulties and mistakes must be conquered by enthusiasm; determination must be sustained by the force of inspiration.

PLATE 3.

VILLAGE NOCTURNE by *Armin Landeck*.

Original size, 10¾ x 8½. Resin-box and Dutch mordant, thirty minutes for deep
blacks; gradation by burnishing and with assistance of drypoint.

(Courtesy of Kennedy & Co.)

Chapter II

MATERIALS EMPLOYED

As time goes on, the artist gradually develops innovations of his own which necessitate the use of materials essential only to himself. There are tools, for example, with which one may be particularly adept and which may eventually be used in connection with any of the aquatint processes, or, for that matter, in any branch of the etching art. I have in mind a dentist I know who uses his electric emery wheel for burnishing small overbitten areas of a copper plate; I, myself, use a certain type of surgical blade for making drypoints. These tools often become necessary for the adequate expression of the individual user.

A list of the standard materials employed in aquatint would include everything used in line etching. For such a list, I refer the student to any of the textbooks on etching in general; Earl H. Reed gives the list which I believe to be most complete in his book, *Etching, A Practical Treatise* (G. P. Putnam's Sons, 1914). A most formidable array of material, but things do accumulate, as every etcher knows.

I shall describe only such materials and preparations as are immediately applicable to aquatint, taking for granted that the student-artist is already familiar with the rest.

Resin Powder. A pound or two of ordinary commercial resin obtained at any painters' supply shop is wrapped in canvas or strong muslin and gently hammered through the cloth into more or less of a fine powder. I say "more or less" because some granules must remain coarse and some even lumpy. About one-quarter of a pound of this powder is placed in a

Dusting Box. Quite a variety of these is described in the textbooks. One wonders whether the more elaborate types are very much in use. I am inclined to believe that most aquatinters employ the simplest sort of device. Briefly, those mentioned are of three types: one where the whole box is made to revolve around an axis at about the middle; one containing a revolving fan operated from the outside; and one into which a set of bellows is used to throw the resin granules into suspension. All are provided with a slide along which a shelf holding the plate is inserted.

The type I myself use is simple and seems to be effective for all purposes. It is a box three feet high and about eighteen inches square, built of thin, light wood, highly polished on the inside, and made thoroughly airtight except for a two-inch aperture on one side near the bottom.

Over this opening is a wooden flap which hermetically closes the box when the shelf is out, and which can be kept in place by a small bolt. The shelf is made to hold a fairly large-sized plate; it slides along grooves or supports on the inner sides of the box, and is edged in front with a two-inch strip of wood that will completely fit into the aperture when the flap is up.

With the shelf out and the flap closed, the resin is shaken into suspension by swinging the whole box over one's head from side to side and then bringing the box down to the floor with a slight thump to prevent any of the granules from clinging to the sides. This action looks to the bystander like a herculean task, yet it is very easily performed because the box is of light construction. Besides, it is good exercise—which even artists need.

Stopping-Out Varnish. The cheapest varnish of the necessary quality is probably French varnish, obtainable at the paint shop. It must be of the finest; if a poor quality is used, it may break down in the acid. French varnish is transparent. If it is not important to see work underneath it, it would be better to mix a little with lampblack in a small porcelain dish to assure a complete stopping-out. Should the varnish become too thick in consistency, the addition of alcohol, a little at a time, will bring it back to normal. Any other stopping-out varnish will do, of course, as long as it is thoroughly acid-resistant.

Brushes. One should be provided with all sizes, including some very fine ones for making thin lines. Sable brushes work best: they are not likely to spread. After they are used they should be well cleaned with alcohol. One can very quickly varnish the back of a plate with a good-sized cotton swab.

Mordants. Some writers recommend nitric acid as strong as fifty per cent for use in aquatint. Far be it from me to lay down specific rules of procedure for any branch of the arts: *art is too flexible to develop under rigid discipline.* But I should advise, in a general way, against the use of any ebullient acid for grain etching, especially when an even tone is desired. The "battery effect" between the closely applied grain must of itself produce irregular biting. If the artist wishes to use nitric, or if no other acid is available, I recommend a solution no stronger than one-third, preferably one-fifth. Constant attention is necessary, and the formation of bubbles "feathered" away on appearance.

An excellent mordant which will give very satisfactory results is ferric chloride, or perchloride of iron. Chemically, its action on the copper is brought about by the formation of hydrochloric acid with the water that held it in

PLATE 5.

FROM THE PONTE VECCHIO by *John Taylor Arms*.

Original size, 11¼ x 15. Aquatint on foreground and pillars placing the note in its proper plane.　　　(*Courtesy of Kennedy & Co.*)

solution. One pound of a saturated aqueous solution is obtained at a chemist's shop; it is diluted with two parts of water; this brings the strength of the original down to one-third and it is then ready for use. Up to a certain point—which varies with temperature and freshness—biting is quite active and even, though unnoticeable; then the formation of a black deposit of iron oxide will inhibit further action of the acid. The deposit is removed by immersing the plate in a very weak solution of hydrochloric acid after which the biting can be resumed in the original bath; for very deep etching I seldom found it necessary to repeat this operation more than twice. Ferric chloride is rapid enough for all purposes and yet operates smoothly; it does not produce so much of the horizontal biting as is likely to occur with nitric acid. Once, on leaving the studio, I forgot a plate in its ferric chloride bath for the final (deep) biting; no doubt the dark iron oxide deposit in the lines prevented the formation of a stencil, for, several hours later when I rushed back I found the effect I had wanted. Nevertheless, I do not in this instance recommend my procedure!

In aquatint, for slow, uniform and certain results the best acid to choose is the mixture of hydrochloric acid and potassium chlorate found in what is known as Smillie's Bath. The formula for this mixture is as follows:

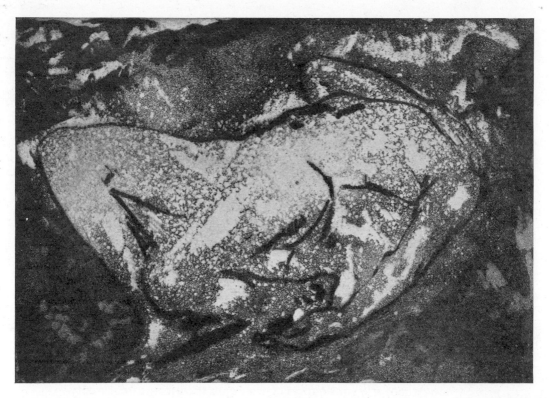

PLATE 6.

TRAGIC FIGURE by *Arthur B. Davies.*

Original size, 6 x 9. Pure aquatint including heavy definition; varied coarse texture obtained by overheating; plate re-aquatinted twice. See Chapter IV. *(Courtesy of Ferargil Galleries)*

Hydrochloric acid .... five ounces
Potassium Chlorate .... one ounce
Water .... twenty-five ounces

To prepare it, dissolve the chlorate of potash in fifteen ounces of warm water, using a quart-sized glass container; allow this to cool and add the other ten ounces of water; then pour the five ounces of chemically pure hydrochloric acid in very slowly, to minimize the heat reaction. When the mixture is cold it is ready for use. Any chemist or pharmacist will prepare the formula, but it may be cheaper to do it oneself. While a plate is in this solution the tray or acid should be frequently agitated to help in the removal of the faint traces of copper chloride that form on the biting area of the plate.

The hydrochloric acid mixture known as Dutch mordant contains the same ingredients as Smillie's Bath except that forty-four ounces of water are used instead of twenty-five. Throughout this book Smillie's Bath is meant whenever hydrochloric acid is mentioned; all other solutions will be specified accordingly.

There is no fixed rule about the use of any mordant. The artist may use any kind or strength of acid that will, in his experience, give the desired result.

Alcohol. Denatured alcohol is the cheapest. It is cheap

16

PLATE 7.

TRIO GYMNASTIQUE by *Dame Laura Knight*.

Original size, 14½ x 10. Deeply bitten fine grain with re-aquatinting
for coarser effects on figures; floodlight evidently burnished out.

(Courtesy of Frederick Keppel & Co.)

enough to use in the form of a bath to remove varnish quickly (French varnish) from the front, back and edges of the plate; or one may use a cotton swab or rag, saturated, for the purpose. The alcohol will also remove the resin ground. Should a wax or asphaltum varnish or ground be used,

Benzine is ideal for its removal. This can be bought cheaply by the gallon in any paint shop. Benzine is practically indispensable to the etcher, and I believe superior to turpentine for cleaning a plate of ink and grease. Turpentine nearly always requires the subsequent use of whiting.

All other materials—such as *roulette, snakestone, sieves, sandpaper, other grounds, acid-resistant crayons, etc.*—will be described as they are mentioned in the chapters that follow.

Chapter III

THE STANDARD METHOD OF PROCEDURE

ONE way to judge whether an already bitten plate should be supported with aquatint is to wipe the inked plate slowly, taking care to leave a tone in those particular places which need it to improve the general composition. If slight tones left by the ink during the printing are sufficient, and can easily be repeated during successive printings, then aquatint support is not at all necessary. The artist should be the sole judge.

It is suggested that the beginner start with a plate requiring simple flat tones only, such as for a sky on a landscape already bitten in line. Snow scenes are admirably suited to this purpose.

Clean the plate thoroughly in the orthodox manner, i.e., with benzine and whiting, and place it face up on the withdrawn shelf of the dusting box. Close the flap of the box. Ordinarily, this would be the signal for a little thinking: what kind of grain is needed, coarse or fine? Is the effect to be light gray, dark gray or black? Is the number of copies to be printed large or small? Do we expect to print in any particular color? But since we are just beginning we shall postpone the consideration of these points until later. We are working for a light gray effect sufficient to throw the snow forward as a pleasing white note in a noontime winter sky.

Drive the resin granules into suspension by swinging the box (one might put handles on it); bring the box to the floor with a thump, or rap on its sides, or rock it. This will prevent too many of the granules from adhering to the interior walls. Wait a few moments to allow the coarser grain to settle, open the flap, and slide in the tray or shelf holding the plate.

When two minutes have passed withdraw the shelf very slowly, breathing very gently—a sneeze would be disastrous—and place it away from draughts. Two minutes are sufficient for an average coat of fine grain texture. If the box contains a large supply of resin powder (one-quarter of a pound) this will do the work. Otherwise, close the flap, shake the box again, and insert the shelf for another minute or two without disturbing the first layer of resin on the plate.

Withdraw the shelf and place on top of the box. Carefully remove the plate without touching the powdered surface—I use a long paper-cutter in one hand and a rag

PLATE 8.

SYMPHONIC POEM by *C. Jac Young*.
   Original size, 7½ x 10. Described in Chapter XIV.   (*Courtesy of Grand Central Art Galleries*)

in the other—and place it on the heated etching stove, holding oneself in readiness to turn the plate at an instant's notice.

If the whole plate rests firmly on an evenly heated stove, the resin grain will assume a brownish, coppery hue over its entire surface at once. At this point the plate should be quickly removed and placed in a cool area of the room, or on the bed of the press, or on the window sill.

However, what usually happens is that the powder turns brown on only part of the plate. This may be due to the uneven heat of the stove, or perhaps to the plate being ever so slightly bent. In any case, the plate must be turned quickly so that the part still showing powdery white is directly over the hottest area of the stove, and just as quickly as this turns brown the plate is moved until the entire resin has been roasted. The whole of this action takes anywhere from a few seconds to half a minute, depending on the heat of the stove—and one must be ever on the alert to prevent overheating. Overheating may melt the resin to the point where it causes all of the granules to coalesce and thereby renders the ground useless.

Incidentally, the object of heating the resin on the copper is to fix it firmly in its form as fine grain, but a certain amount of coalescence is unavoidable and frequently gives

22

PLATE 9.

SILENT NIGHT by *R. W. Woiceske.*

　　Original size, 10 x 15. Coarse grain sky giving the snow its relative value.

(Courtesy of Kleemann Galleries)

us a coarser texture of grain than what we originally intended. Also, the heating is a true roasting process in that dehydration takes place, rendering the ground very hard —much harder than the ordinary etching ground; this is quite advantageous, as we shall see later on. A resin-grounded plate can be carried safely with no more protection than a paper envelope.

After fixing and cooling, completely stop out everything on the plate that is not to be toned. The varnish will have a tendency to spread; the excess on the brush should be removed before use. Placing the plate on a large piece of cardboard will facilitate the turning of it during the stopping-out. Large plates are conveniently handled by placing them on a revolving stool so that nothing will be upset while turning. (These suggestions are offered now for use later when various parts of the plate are to be alternatingly stopped-out and bitten a number of times.) The edges and back are also to be varnished as in any other etching.

When thoroughly dry, place in Smillie's Bath at ordinary room temperature for thirty seconds; if the acid is old, for longer. One may follow the biting-time shown in Test Plate I. The plate is then washed with water and cleaned with alcohol and benzine, and we are now ready for a trial proof—a thrilling moment that never cloys.

Standard Method of Procedure

If more than one area on the plate needs aquatinting, I recommend that this be postponed until further chapters of this book have been read.

So that the beginner will more easily follow the successive steps of obtaining a light gray area of aquatint, I briefly review the procedure as I have just described it:

1. Keep perfectly cool.
2. Clean plate thoroughly.
3. Place it on withdrawn shelf of resin box.
4. With flap closed, shake the box and bring it to the floor with vigor.
5. Open flap and insert shelf holding plate.
6. Wait two minutes and withdraw shelf; breathe gently.
7. Carefully lift plate off shelf with long paper or palette knife and place on heated stove.
8. Fix with great care as described.
9. When cool, varnish out all areas not to be toned; also back and edges of plate.
10. Place in Smillie's Bath for thirty seconds to two minutes, depending on tone required, or in ferric chloride bath for thirty seconds, or in nitric acid (thirty-three per cent) bath for ten seconds.
11. Quickly and thoroughly rinse and clean the plate.

Chapter IV

RULES OF GROUNDING

THE action of acids, the type of grain, the biting-time, the quality of copper, the temperature and humidity of the weather—all these involve laws of physics and chemistry that one cannot entirely ignore and must keep consciously in mind at all times.

We can make fixed rules relating to the biting-time and the type of grain used in aquatint only if we have definite knowledge of the exact action of the acid and the resistance of the metal plate. I do not mean we should be too technical. I don't expect that any artist is going to figure out the molecular weight of the alloy in any particular plate and then study the barometer and the thermometer. That would certainly take the joy out of artistic inspiration.

For practical purposes, therefore, we shall consider the copper plate—I do not recommend zinc for aquatints—purchased at the art store as the average in hardness, and the chemically pure acid of the chemist's as the average

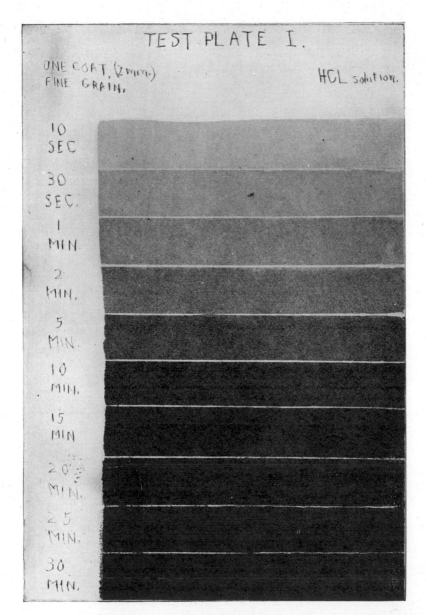

PLATE 10.

TEST PLATE I.

Original size same as reproduction. Discussed in Chapters IV., V., VII. and XII.

in biting power in a room temperature of seventy degrees, Fahrenheit.

The biting-time charted in Test Plate I was made with a fresh solution of Smillie's Bath on a two-minute coating of fine grain from the newly replenished dusting box. Each number designates the total biting-time of its respective area. In the same way, Test Plate II was made with two such coats of powdered resin, thus giving a very coarse grain effect. A clean wipe was used in the printing of these plates and the reproductions are in the exact sizes of the originals.

From these illustrations it can readily be seen that the more powder one puts on the plate the less exposed copper remains to be bitten, and, therefore, the coarser is the texture produced. Expressing it the other way round, the less powder one puts on the plate the more exposed copper remains to be bitten, thereby increasing the tone value.

This, however, is true only within certain limits, for if we were to carry either process to its extreme we should obtain negative results. That is, if we add enough powder to cover the entire plate completely no biting would take place, and, conversely, if we reach the point where no powder is added at all the plate would be evenly bitten (theoretically), so that no ink could be held for the printing.

28

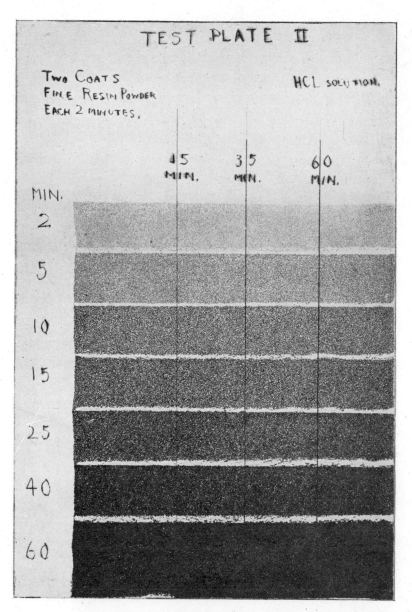

PLATE II.

TEST PLATE II.

Original size same as reproduction. Discussed in Chapters IV., V., VII. and XI.

When we have a thorough understanding of the relationship between the bitten and the unbitten parts of the plate that form the aquatint area, we can reduce everything to simple formulæ that will serve as guides for future action.

Since the resin granules are acid-resistant, that part of the plate which they cover will still remain the original surface of the copper; we will call this the *surface area*. The part of the plate surrounding each granule, being unprotected, is therefore attacked by the acid; we will call this the *bitten area*.

Let me repeat what I have already suggested in other words: *The greater the surface area in relation to bitten area, the coarser is the textural effect.*

As we increase the surface area (by adding more powder) we gradually lose out on tonal value, that "wash-drawing" effect of aquatint. For it must be remembered that the bitten area holds ink both for texture and tone, and should these etched receptacles get to be too far apart only texture will remain and tone will have disappeared. Such a result is not what we are seeking. We must, therefore, prevent tone and texture from parting company. Roughly, this is done by adding not much more than two three-minute coats of powdered resin from the freshly supplied dusting box.

30

It follows that when the surface area is exactly equal to the bitten area, the relationship of tone and texture is the closest. Theoretically, that gives us a perfect aquatint—which may or may not be desired; its quality depends on the size and shape of the grain. Even here, however, it is not desirable to have too large a grain, for again we begin to lose out on tonal value as the textural effect increases in coarseness.

From this point we can carry our deduction to the other extreme. If it is possible to have texture without tone, it is also possible to obtain tone without texture—at least a grain texture. Actually this is as much pure theory as my previous statement about the acid attacking the entire free surface of the copper and leaving no tone in the printing; most etchers have had experience with accidental biting such as this and found it to be irregular enough to present texture and tone.

At some time, though, texture does begin to part with tone, as the bitten area increases in size over the surface area, so that finally we lose the grain effect that is also essential to aquatint. To prevent this, we apply not less than half of our standard coat of powdered resin; in short, we leave the plate in the box for forty-five seconds instead of two minutes, assuming that most of the suspended granules settle within that time.

That leads us to another rule—and its converse—which we must remember: *The coarser the texture becomes the more we lose in tonal value,* and, *The finer the texture becomes the more we gain in tonal value.*

This brings us to the further consideration of how a coarse grain texture is produced. One method has already been described: to increase the amount of fine powder on the plate—provided that more than half the total area was originally covered. Another way is to increase the size of the resin grains; if these are already in the dusting box they can readily be caught by inserting the plate immediately after suspension and withdrawing it after about forty seconds, or before the finer grains had a chance to settle. As this obviously is an insufficient covering, the process is repeated several times (four times for forty seconds each in Test Plate III).

A coarser texture can also be attained by intentionally overheating the plate during the fixing of the resin grain, thereby increasing the amount of coalescence. This must be done with great caution and the plate examined under a strong magnifying glass before etching it in order to make certain that a complete stopping-out has not occurred; if one doesn't make sure, the subsequent tedious proceedings of stopping-out and biting may prove to be love's labor lost.

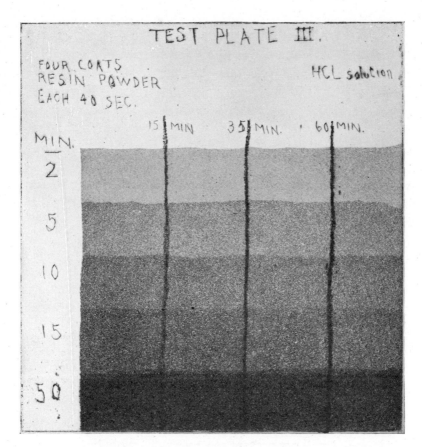

PLATE 12.

TEST PLATE III.

Original size same as reproduction. Discussed in Chapters IV. and V.

Various types of sieves are probably employed more often than dusting boxes for the application of resin powder onto a copper plate. These—either of wire or cloth— can be made to apply any size of grain by successive filtering and transferring from one sieve to another. The field of operation must be so prepared that all draughts are avoided. The plate is best placed on the floor and surrounded by a piece of cardboard or wrapping paper about the size and form of a flour barrel; hold the sieve about three feet above the plate. The sieve (or box) is tapped and shaken gently to bring about a more or less even shower. One can use a barrel, of course, but the bottom should be removed so that the plate can be reached without disturbing its powdered coating.

For varying textures, box, sieve, and hand-sprinkling are resorted to in combination.

At this point it is worth considering the size of the edition one wishes to print from the aquatinted plate. Steelfacing, as we know, usually solves this problem. Even this, however, will not prevent some very delicately bitten areas from wearing down early, and besides, not a few artists are peculiarly averse to steelfacing.

Steeled or not, some aquatints do not hold up as well as others, a puzzling incident indeed, and sometimes disappointing. It may be because the metal of some copper

34

plates is too pure and hence softer. Strangely enough this wearing down is not entirely due to shallowness of the receptacles, though, obviously, weak biting does remain an important factor.

The explanation lies again in the relationship between the surface area and the bitten area. Visualize an aquatinted plate as consisting of minute hills (surface area) within an immense valley (bitten area). If these hills are small (fine grain) they can be more easily wiped and pressed down to the level of the valley than if they had broad plateaus (large grain).

In other words: *The coarser the texture the larger is the edition of good prints,* other things being equal.

Chapter V

RULES OF ETCHING

IN Test Plate II, before the resin was applied, three vertical lines were etched in slightly warmed hydrochloric acid (Smillie's Bath) for fifteen, thirty-five, and sixty minutes respectively, in order to show what happens to these during continued biting with the grain ground.

Note how the finest line begins to disappear as the aquatint receptacles become deeper and wider. The minute granules that had rested on the edges of the groove of this line naturally broke up its continuity and at the same time the line itself was irregularly deepened and widened. This would have been further manifested were the lines etched on Test Plate I where a finer grain texture was used. The same thing would have occurred had the lines been drypoint, in which case the burr would have been equally attacked by the acid and the lines softened considerably.

We have, then, the following rules to bear in mind: *Lines change in quality and intensity as aquatint biting advances. The finer the grain texture the more readily do lines soften and disappear under aquatint biting.*

36

PLATE 13.

BROADCASTING STATION by *George O. "Pop" Hart.*

Original size, 7⅛ x 8⅞. Softground and some drypoint followed by irregular application of grain from dust-bag and hand sprinkling.   (*Courtesy of Downtown Gallery*)

The contrast between lines and grain in their relation-ship to tonal value becomes less and less as the biting progresses until complete fusion takes place. Should the biting be continued indefinitely, both lines and grain tex-ture would eventually disappear in a mutilated copper plate, for the hydrochloric acid not only bites vertically but also horizontally—the latter direction to greater ex-tent when nitric acid is used—and, at some time, the minute hills are leveled to the base of the valley, giving us neither lines nor aquatint.

Hence, Test Plate I, containing a fine grain, was bitten only as long as thirty minutes, the receptacles being much closer together than those in Test Plate II. The fine recep-tacles might have fused if the biting had been continued longer, in which event they would have been too large to retain the ink during the wiping of the plate and they would have printed as grayish in tone, lacking in effectual texture.

On Test Plate I the maximum tone intensity was reached in fifteen minutes of biting-time. A further biting of fifteen minutes failed to result in any perceptible fusion, at least to the naked eye; that leaves a rather wide margin of safety. Also, as I brought out in the last chapter, the increased biting gives a greater ruggedness and that in turn is necessary if one wants a large edition of good prints. On Test Plate II, since the receptacles were both

CRONIES by *Martin Lewis*.

Original size, 9⅞ x 11. Grain applied with sieve; re-aquatinted twice; Dutch mordant used.   (*Courtesy of Kennedy & Co.*)

wider and farther apart, there was no hesitancy in continuing the biting for one hour; in this case the danger of fusion is much less.

For practical purposes, therefore, let us remember: *The coarser the grain the further can biting progress without loss of texture.*

This rule, of course, applies only to the texture of the original state of the surface area. Actually and progressively, it will be noticed on both of these two test plates that the texture changed with each successive bite; this can be spotted more easily with the coarser grain. The reason is obviously the increasing size of the bitten area brought about by horizontal biting; the result is not only deepened tones but distinct losses in textural effects. On Test Plate II, for example, one can see more white in the ten-minute area than in the sixty-minute area.

Therefore: *Continued biting reduces the textural effect and increases the tonal value.*

One might continue with further observations and theories on these two test plates, but I shall mention only one more interesting feature regarding relative values. In the case of line, one knows that the deeper it is engraved into the copper the darker it will be in print. In aquatint this principle is modified by the changes in the grain. Compare the fifteen-minute area of Test Plate I with the

PLATE 15.

STOOPS IN SNOW by *Martin Lewis*.

Original size, 10 x 15. Same technique as PLATE 14.

(Courtesy of Kennedy & Co.)

sixty-minute area of Test Plate II. Notwithstanding the fact that the latter was bitten four times as long, the former is nevertheless darker in tone. This vast difference in biting-time further accentuates the rule discussed in the last chapter, that the finer the grain the richer is the tone even though both areas hold about the same amount of ink. This is important to remember when looking for rich tonal values in relation to biting-time.

In softground etching the texture of the paper—or cloth —that lifts the ground is imparted to the lines, and the depth of these lines is influenced by the pressure and quality of the pencil or other tool employed. We are dealing with a grain-like structure and, for this reason, the lines blend so perfectly with aquatint that were they lightly etched they would readily disappear under deep aquatint biting. Test Plate III contains three vertical lines etched with softground in warm hydrochloric acid for fifteen, thirty-five and sixty minutes respectively. The lines were made with a thick, soft pencil pressed twice over the paper. Though there is not much difference of intensity between the lines on the clear area of copper, the degree of blending of each line manifestly differs as the biting advances. Here is a texture of grain somewhat similar to that employed on Test Plate II, yet it is obtained in a different manner: immediately after suspension of the powder the plate was inserted in the resin box four times for forty seconds. Had I used a fine texture, the softground lines would have more readily blended with the grain.

With average biting-time these lines become very materially changed, and sometimes are actually accentuated, particularly under a light coating of resin powder. The reason for this is the continued biting of uncovered portions of line. This interesting phenomenon can be prevented by inking these lines and wiping the surface of the copper thoroughly clean before the application of the resin ground; in this way the ink acts as a mild deterrent to the action of the acid until the biting is over.

For strong definition of grained masses the deeply etched softground line is the most sympathetic of all lines. As guides, even when lightly etched, they are easily seen under the resin ground, and the process of stopping-out up to definition is more neatly accomplished than with the comparatively stiff hardground etched line. Softground and aquatint make an ideal combination. With this in mind, and in order that the significance of the grain effect of softground etching may be more fully appreciated in its relationship to aquatint, I feel justified in reviewing the technique of softground etching in the following chapter.

Chapter VI

THE TEXTURAL EFFECTS OF
SOFTGROUND ETCHING

WHY any process of etching a line into a copper plate should be regarded with disfavor just because it bears a resemblance to another medium is something I have always failed to understand. No true artist could possibly disregard a method of expression which exactly interprets his artistic mood. I have frequently heard the remark that softground etching is a method employed to imitate the effect of a lithograph, which, even if true, is not by itself a valid reason for disuse. At any rate, I most assuredly do not agree with this opinion, for softground is as beautiful and expressive as any other medium. Our main interest at present, however, lies in its frequent use as an important accompaniment to aquatint.

The materials employed consist of soft etching ground, a variety of more or less thin tracing paper and pencils of varying quality.

The ground can usually be purchased already prepared at most shops selling artists' supplies. It can also be made

44

PLATE 16.

IRRESISTIBLE CALL by *Lewis C. Daniel*.

Original size, 7½ x 10. Softground etching showing quality of line easily blended with aquatint
(Chapters V. and VI.). *(Courtesy of Grand Central Art Galleries)*

quite simply by mixing regular etching ground with tallow in varying proportions, depending on the season's temperature. The ground is melted over a slow fire in any kind of metal container, preferably placed in a larger receptacle partly filled with water; the tallow is added slowly and mixed until an even consistency is obtained. Care must be taken that the heating does not progress more than is necessary to accomplish the desired result, otherwise the mixture may be burnt to brittleness. In the cold weather months, equal parts of etching ground and tallow are mixed; in the warmer months the amount of tallow is reduced to one-third of the whole. The new ground is now rapidly cooled by scooping it up with a spoon or ladle and plunging it into cold water. Before hardness is reached it is molded into a ball and wrapped in silk. Then it is ready for use.

In general, the paper is of thin, translucent material containing a textural surface, or what is known as "teeth." It is surprising how many papers of an apparent smoothness are adaptable to the purpose after being dampened. One can use heavier paper, providing the ground will not be injured, but thin tracing paper is most suitable—a sketch can be transferred on it very easily. There are some forms of bond paper that also do quite well. Examining the grain or texture with a magnifying glass will give the artist a good idea of what results may be expected. The masters have used various cloths of silk and linen for interesting textures; such effects are impossible to duplicate by the lithographic stone. It offers a tremendous field for future experimentation.

Different types of pencils give different results. Pencils should be hard, medium and soft, sharp-pointed and flat-edged, thick and thin. To make the subject much simpler, one can make a complete softground etching with the use of only one pencil, or any other blunt instrument. It all depends on what the artist wants. The pencil markings have nothing to do with the final result; they do, however, serve to show one's drawing in the *positive* as one proceeds, although in reverse of the final print.

To proceed, apply the soft ground to the plate just as is done in "straight" etching, either with dabber or roller. I personally prefer the dabber. Some artists smoke the ground in order that they may the more easily see how it is lifting as they progress. Smoking the ground hardens it slightly, an advantage in very hot weather. Care must be taken that the surface of the plate is never touched by hand or other irrelevant material as the ground is easily bruised. To prevent accidents, the grounded plate is placed in an etching tray over the edges of which some sort of shelf is set for the hand to rest on. A bridge-like mechanism can be constructed, instead, of a board four inches wide and about a foot long supported by a block of wood along each edge; this is a useful article for any kind of etching.

Meanwhile, the sketch or outline, dependent upon the purpose required, is traced with ink or pencil on the paper which should be larger in every direction than the size of the plate. To the more or less experienced it may not be necessary to observe the progress of the "lift," in which case one side of the paper is dampened with a sponge and neatly folded over the grounded plate, pasting all ends on the back of the copper with paper adhesive tape and allowed to dry. If one is interested, however, in observing the "lift," the plate is anchored on a drawing board with thumb tacks and the paper placed over it and fixed in similar manner. In either case one must approximate the position of the sketch on the plate over the desired area.

At this point, it is best to bear in mind that the object of this procedure is to make the ground adhere firmly to the paper wherever pressure is applied so that the copper is bared sufficiently for the action of the acid. With the assistance of the hand-shelf the pencil is firmly—and with confidence—pressed over the lines of the sketch, care being taken that the paper is not torn. Progress can be

PLATE 17.

MÈRE ET ENFANT DANS LES BRAS by *Mary Cassatt*.

Original size, 8½ x 5½. Aquatint in support of line; softground etching; grain applied with dust-bag.   (*Courtesy of Frederick Keppel & Co.*)

watched by lifting up a corner or side of the paper which in turn lifts off the plate with reluctance; the lines or masses of copper surface are looked at to determine whether sufficient pressure is being used and the paper returned to its former position for further work. Sometimes, especially when the ground is smoked, the etcher may be mistaken as to the completeness of the "lift": actually, either through insufficient pressure or due to the unaccountable resistance of the ground, a thin film of coating may remain on the plate; this will inhibit the action of the acid. The sheen of the copper must be definitely seen.

Varied effects can now be obtained by the proper use of the different kinds of pencils. It is suggested that definitions be made with the hard pencils and shadings with the soft. One may even press the paper firmly with the thumb, but this must be neatly done otherwise the effect may look too smudgy.

It is not necessary, of course, to have a sketch previously prepared. One may use a totally blank sheet of paper and spontaneously improvise a composition, perhaps a portrait or a landscape. The advantage of the medium, as stated before, is that it is a positive process and that the lines or masses can be made to possess almost any kind of textural quality.

RHYTHM ORIENTAL by *Frank A. Nankivell.*

Original size, 10 x 8. Brilliant example of mixed methods; definition of dancing figures etched by positive pen process; straight aquatint on figures and ground; aquatint and mezzotint on dancing master; lift ground, Hamerton's emulsion, on foliage. *(Courtesy of Ferargil Galleries)*

When satisfied that the sketch is completed, the paper is carefully removed, all errors are varnished out, as well as the back and edges of the plate. It is suggested that all parts of the ground free of lines also be varnished to prevent any false biting that may occur in the weak areas. The plate is then ready for the acid bath.

Most rules applicable to biting an aquatint hold equally well for softground since both processes require the breaking up of a resistant ground in a granular manner for the purpose of producing a tonal and textural effect. The only change is in the biting-time because, as I have already said, there remains always an extremely thin layer of ground which is never entirely removed by the paper even though the sheen of the copper is readily seen; this layer temporarily inhibits the action of the hydrochloric acid. Stopping-out for successive bitings must be made carefully, as there is always danger of injuring the ground with the brush.

Further work on a softground etching is generally done on the unsmoked ground either by using a new (very thin) sheet of tracing paper or by superimposing the original sheet on the plate. For the latter method, it should be remembered that the paper, if dampened, slightly distorts the sketch by expanding; this makes approximation awkward. It is suggested that in either method the plate be inked and wiped clean before regrounding so that all previous work can be more clearly seen. Other correctional measures can be made with the roulette wheel, or even with the drypoint needle, and the burr removed. The printing of the plate is the same as for any other etching.

Chapter VII

PRINTING AN AQUATINT

FUNDAMENTALLY, the rules for printing an aquatint are practically the same as those employed for any
other type of engraving. There are, however, a few additional items to consider. Each plate presents its own char-
acteristics, with which the printer soon becomes familiar.
Broadly speaking, the consistency of the ink is thinned
as the biting is advanced, but this is a matter upon which
to use one's own judgment, based on general printing
experience.

I shall take as my starting point an average example of
pure aquatint, or aquatint plus softground, or aquatint
plus "pure" line etching. The plate is inked while heated
and then allowed to cool; meanwhile excess ink is removed by gently wiping the plate with a "fatty" rag.
When the plate is cold, the wiping is continued with
rapid circular motions, using tarlatan or any mosquito-
netting type of cloth.

If a thoroughly clean wipe is desired—so that the texture will show clearly—the rag is heated on the stove for

a moment and then run rapidly over the cold plate; this is repeated several times. Frequently, the palm, aided by whiting, is used to wipe with, even in aquatinted plates.

By examining Test Plates I and II once again, it is possible to observe that the depth of biting, regardless of the amount or quality of grain, has a decided relationship to the tone produced in the printing. The grain texture is not so easily discernible in the lightly bitten areas as it is in the more deeply etched parts. This, of course, is due, respectively, to the gray-and-white and the black-and-white contrasts. It follows, then, that if ink were left on the surface area of these lightly bitten parts of the plate the grain texture would be still less manifest, possibly distinguishable only with a magnifying glass.

Grain texture is frequently eliminated in printing strongly bitten aquatint areas, when the artist is interested only in solid blacks. In this case the tone is not left on the plate in the usual way, i.e., by not wiping the ink entirely off the surface area; smudges would be likely to appear on the print if one were to do that. The plate is first wiped fairly clean and then evenly retroussaged by coaxing the ink out of the receptacles over the surface area with a soft rag (cheese-cloth) on the warm plate just before placing it on the bed of the press for the imprint.

What may present some difficulty in printing is the

55

combination of aquatint and drypoint. It is the burr, of course, which interferes. In the print the burr produces an inartistic appearance, especially when deep drypoint serves as the definition for lightly bitten aquatint, each normally requiring a different consistency of ink. This burr should be scraped out, or at least down. However, where burr is sometimes used to bolster up a deeply bitten area it aids considerably in carrying the ink necessary for a solid black; the combination results in a velvety blackness almost similar to mezzotint.

Often the note of a composition is wiped clean, the rest of the plate gradating away into darkness; this treatment depends on the plate and on the individual preference of the artist. It must always be remembered that aquatint is a black-and-white painting and that any kind of wiping which will give the desired effect should be employed. If it is necessary to accentuate the whiteness of a particular area or note, palm wiping with whiting is used; if the area is too small for that, the finger, or even a paper matchstick, will prove efficient in removing excess ink.

After many impressions have been taken, all the variously bitten areas will begin to wear down, the numerous little hilltops will have had their edges rounded off, and the result will be a softness in tone and texture in the print. This may not by any means be undesirable, in spite

PLATE 19.
STILL LIFE WITH CRANACH PAINTING by *Emil Ganso*.
Original size, 11⅞ x 10. Plate grounded four times with resin-box for varied
texture; mordant, nitric acid fifty per cent. (*Courtesy of Weyhe Gallery*)

of a slight loss of that "brilliancy" in the impression. The ink must be made more tenacious as the aquatint wears down, otherwise it will be wiped off too easily.

The most lightly bitten areas, of the finest texture, are the first to weaken. One hopes that the complete edition will have been printed when this occurs; normally, with about thirty prints, the plate can be regarded as having rendered fair service. Should more good prints be called for and no amount of retroussage proves satisfactory, a second state of the plate, not dissimilar to the first, can be made by re-aquatinting. This is best done by completely burnishing out the weakened area, and then applying approximately the same grain as before. The memory often can be assisted by examining closely a first-state impression.

Contrary to the general opinion, some aquatints do hold up splendidly for large editions. I have seen many plates used for one hundred prints each, without steelfacing, and the last print turned out to be as good as the first.

I suggest that the plate be perfectly cleaned after every few impressions. It sometimes happens that the paper will not take the ink from certain portions; it usually means that the ink mixture has hardened and dried in the receptacles, in which case it will not have been noticed during the inking and wiping.

Chapter VIII

OTHER FORMS OF AQUATINT

AQUATINT is a grain process of etching for the production of tone and texture. The name suggested itself because of the resemblance of the print to a wash drawing. Any type of grain employed, therefore, that will give this effect rightfully belongs to the general classification of aquatint, although it has been the custom of some writers in the past to regard the process as specific to the resin grain. These writers referred to the use of all other grain substances as allied processes. It is my opinion that we should apply the term aquatint, whatever the grain, in order to avoid confusion, except perhaps in a technical discussion of a particular print. When we are being technical the specificity of grain may be designated in a hyphenated manner, such as salt-aquatint, or sand-aquatint, or sulphur-aquatint.

The oldest form of aquatint is the *sulphur-aquatint* used by many of the experimentally inclined etchers (including Rembrandt) of the seventeenth century. The procedure is as follows: Clean the plate entirely of moisture, grease and tarnish. The tarnish (chemically, copper oxide if brown and copper chloride if green) may be removed by rubbing with a mixture of salt and vinegar. With a brush, paint the area to be toned with pure olive oil and over this dust precipitated sulphur powder, commonly called Flowers of Sulphur. The powder may conveniently be placed in a saltcellar. Wipe off any grain or oil that may have fallen elsewhere on the plate, and let the plate stand for several hours. The exact time is not of great consequence since the biting is self-limiting. This may be repeated, using a coarser (*less* of the powder) ground at each successive application; always clean the plate before the application.

At best, this aquatint is not very deep and has very little grain texture. It does, however, possess a tone which resembles a wash drawing more than any other grain etching; it will not hold up for very many prints. The old masters used the sulphur-aquatint to support a closely cross-hatched line etching in obtaining a more solid tone.

Incidentally, it will be remarked that in connection with the sulphur grain—and also with salt and sand—I refer to a coarser grain as consisting of fewer granules; it is just the reverse in the case of resin. The biting with the resin ground takes place around each granule; with salt, sand and sulphur the biting takes place where the

60

PLATE 20.

THE NEW YORK PUBLIC LIBRARY by *Edith Nankivell.*

Original size, 7 x 10. Line etching and sandpaper aquatint described in Chapter VIII.

(Courtesy of Cronyn & Lowndes Galleries)

granules *are* or *were*. In other words, the hill-valley idea of the resin-aquatint now gives way to an appearance under the magnifying glass of innumerable little craters in a huge flat surface area. The fewer of these craters the coarser will be the texture.

Still another effective method for the application of the sulphur ground is to use the mixture as a paint. Pound and mix two parts of bay-salt with one part sal ammoniac and one part verdigris; keep this in a wide-necked glass bottle. When in use, a little of this mixture is ground up with syrup of old honey, and the emulsion thus made is painted onto the copper with a brush. From here on, the process is about the same as that I have just described: let it stand for several hours, etc.

About 1773 there appeared the first published description of the *salt process of aquatint* by the Frenchman, M. Stapart. Briefly, his method can be simplified to what follows: Grind up into slightly smaller grains the commercial sea-salt obtainable at the pharmacist's, and place the grains in a coarsely perforated salt-shaker. Cover the plate with ordinary hard etching ground and dab thin; keep the ground in the hot semi-liquid state and shake the salt over it freely. Take the usual precaution of not getting the ground too hot, in order that it may not burn and become brittle. The salt grains will precipitate to the sur-

PLATE 21.

"DEBUSSY" No. 1. by *Frank A. Nankivell.*

Original size, 7 x 5. Irregularly applied spirit ground for varied texture (Chapter VIII.); some corrections made with roulette and drypoint.

(Courtesy of Leonard Clayton Gallery)

face of the plate, and when satisfied that enough has been added for the desired effect, allow the plate to cool slowly by placing it in warm water; this will dissolve the salt. When cold and dry, stop-out and etch in the usual way. As far as I know the salt-aquatint is no longer used except, perhaps, experimentally.

The *sand process of aquatint* is not usually employed in the form of free granules, although I see no reason why this cannot be done in the same way as the sea-salt. The sand particles may not all wash away in the water bath, but this does not make much difference as the acid will find its way to the plate surface just the same.

The practiced method is to apply the grain attached to sandpaper. Apply the hard etching ground, leave unsmoked, and allow to cool. Reduce the pressure of the press, place the plate on the bed face up, and cover completely with one sheet of sandpaper face down. Both are then run through the rollers. Edith Nankivell, daughter of the master-aquatinter, did this eight times in the accompanying illustration, using a fresh piece of sandpaper for each "pull" and placing it over the plate in a different position to avoid a possible "grain direction." By this time the ground was sufficiently broken up to give a fine grained texture. For coarser effects, the number of pulls is reduced, though obviously this depends on the make used.

64

PLATE 22.

THE SONG by *Eugene C. Fitsch.*

    Original size, 7¾ x 6½. Line etching for base and definition; coarse grain on figure and fine grain for background applied with dust-bag.

(Courtesy of Morton Gallery)

Good results may also be obtained by using coarse emery paper; but this, however, may prove expensive. The plate is now ready to be bitten after the necessary stopping-out.

The early aquatinters used a liquid ground, or what is more aptly referred to as a *spirit ground* to differentiate it from the liquid ground used in line etching. A stock solution is first prepared by dissolving about five ounces of resin powder in a pint of rectified spirits (alcohol, ninety-five per cent); this is shaken periodically for several hours and allowed to stand for a few days. Then the clear solution is decanted and the impure residue thrown away. From this solution an amount necessary for the desired effect is mixed with a fresh pint of alcohol: about five ounces for a fine grain aquatint, and relatively more for coarser results. All bottles are labeled with the exact formulae of the contents.

The required solution is poured evenly over the surface of the copper and allowed to evaporate. The resin eventually precipitates in a very fine reticulation, imparting, after biting, an almost perfect wash-drawing effect to the print.

Asphaltum can be used in place of resin, either as a powder or as spirit ground. The two gums are sometimes mixed in varying proportion, but I can see no superior advantage in any kind of such combination for aquatint.

In fixing the asphaltum grain to the copper over the heater, the reddish-brown color of this gum turns to blue which is the indication that the fixing is accomplished.

Various other combinations have been used in the past, and are included in the following list offered by T. H. Fielding (in 1844). I present it only for its academic interest:

1. Turpentine varnish dissolved in alcohol,
2. Burgundy pitch and resin, equal parts,
3. Burgundy pitch alone,
4. Resin alone,
5. Mastic and Burgundy pitch, equal parts,
6. Mastic alone,
7. Frankincense alone,
8. Mastic and common resin.

Chapter IX

THE LIFT GROUND

IN any branch of the etching art (for that matter in any thing at all!) undue accidents should be carefully avoided —with stress on the word *undue*. Accidents are seldom of any value, though I admit that in art there are some that actually do improve the compositions in which they occur.

Nevertheless, the accident in art is not the thing to be sought, in spite of the welcoming attitude of some artists. One may become satisfied with something that was not originally a personal expression, and art is essentially a personal expression.

There are such things, however, as strange qualities of texture and tone in aquatint resulting from many uncontrollable forces, and if these are to be called accidental it must be admitted that they are at least *incidental* to the process employed. Paradoxically, they may be regarded as unforeseen and yet not entirely unexpected.

This is what makes the "lift ground" in aquatint so very fascinating. The method is similar, technically, to the brush process of etching described by P. G. Hamer-

PLATE 23.

SIDE STREET by *Albert Heckman.*

Original size, 9 x 12¼. Described in Chapter IX. *(Courtesy of Ferargil Galleries)*

ton in 1881, except for the addition of the resin ground. Briefly, a plate is thoroughly cleaned and resin-grounded; directly upon this the sketch is made with Hamerton's emulsion; liquid ground is then poured over the entire plate and the whole immersed in a Dutch mordant bath.

These are the details of the procedure: Prepare the emulsion by first adding an amount of ordinary etcher's whiting in a saturated solution of white sugar (simple syrup) to make an easy flowing suspension about the consistency of stopping-out varnish. Add ox-gall in an amount equivalent to half of this mixture. Ox-gall is usually sold as a powder but it should not be used in this form as the entire emulsion may be rendered too thick for use. Shake the mixture well before using; it also should be tested for proper consistency by trying it out with a brush on the back of the plate. If it is too thick, add water or more ox-gall; if it is too thin, add more whiting or place some in a small porcelain dish and let it stand until it is fit.

On a plate resin-grounded to a desired texture draw the sketch with the emulsion, using a very fine sable brush. Apply thick or thin depending on values required, using water as a diluent, bearing in mind that the thicker the paste applied to any area the blacker will that area print. To make the method a more positive process, I

PLATE 24.

KNITTING by *Joseph Margulies.*
Original size, 10½ x 7. Lift ground; technique similar to PLATE 23.

(Courtesy of Weyhe Gallery)

suggest that lampblack be substituted for some of the whiting used in making the emulsion.

It is convenient to use small porcelain or glass dishes for the emulsion and the water, and to paint as one does on canvas with oil and turpentine (except that in this case the plate lies horizontally on the table). Any errors can be diluted away, but this must be done quite thoroughly because traces of the paste will affect the action of the acid. So that the paste will "stay put," and not "draw up," a little saliva may be used—although this effect should be achieved by the ox-gall, if a sufficient amount has been added.

The next step is important. The usual liquid ground is made by dissolving an ounce of hard etching ground in eight ounces of ether. This should be thin enough for use here, but some grounds being harder than others it may be necessary to add more ether. The ether will probably have to be added if the artist uses an old solution. With great care—and pipe laid aside, ether being highly inflammable—the liquid is poured over the resin-grounded plate containing the sketch, once and only once; the excess is tilted off back into the bottle. I repeat, the ground should be very thin, thin enough so that when it becomes hard and somewhat brittle the sketch underneath should be able to throw it off easily.

72

PLATE 25.

BETWEEN MOVES by *Joseph Margulies*.
Original size, 10 x 7½. Lift ground; technique similar to PLATE 23.

(Courtesy of Weyhe Gallery)

The ex-liquid ground has settled in the interstices of the resin granules and has completely stopped-out everything but the sketch. As a matter of precaution this stopping-out should be supported with varnish. In the meanwhile, the sketch has prevented the liquid ground from penetrating to the free surface area of the copper—the thicker the paste on any area the more it stops the liquid; where the emulsion is thinly applied minute penetration occurs proportionately.

The ether is allowed to evaporate completely before placing the plate in the Dutch mordant bath. This is a much weaker solution of hydrochloric acid than we have been using thus far, the formula being approximately as follows:

Hydrochloric Acid, C. P........five ounces
Potassium Chlorate.............one ounce
Water....................forty-four ounces

After about fifteen minutes in the bath, the "straight" ground covering the sketch begins to break and lift off in proportion to the amount of paste underneath it; the paste follows. This action can be hastened by gently swabbing with cotton or brushing with a feather. The biting is allowed to continue to the desired extent. The average time is forty-five minutes.

The chances are that further work will be necessary,

74

burnishing and probably re-aquatinting in the ordinary manner, but the ground work has been laid for effects undoubtedly never thought of, and the etcher will find the game well worth the candle.

The ingredients of the emulsion as given are those used by Hamerton. I present it as a starting point for future development, as I have seen some brilliant examples of lift-ground aquatints which were made with various modifications and improvements of his formula. In fact, some have differed so radically that nothing of the original formula remains. The idea is to obtain a tenacious mixture (although not as tenacious as etching ground) and at the same time one non-resistant to the acid yet temporarily acting as a deterrent. It is preferable that this paste, or emulsion, or suspension, be alkaline in reaction; this, however, is not necessary provided that the mixture is at least chemically neutral. It can be seen that biting a plate with such a paste on it renders the acid hardly fit for further use.

The method of procedure just described is the one used by Nankivell and Heaslip in the plates *Rhythm Oriental* and *The Next Hop*. Of late years, however, the European aquatinters, notably the French, have used a modification and variation of the foregoing routine; it gives equally good results but varies somewhat in textural effects. The aquatints of Margulies and Heckman are of this type.

In this latter process the sketch is painted directly on the bare copper surface which may or may not be first prepared by dipping it for a few seconds in a weak solution of acid to keep the applied suspension from buckling or drawing up. The liquid ground is then poured on, after the sketch is dry, and the lift provoked by placing the whole in water. When this is completed and the plate is dried, the resin ground is applied in the usual manner.

I personally believe the first procedure is superior to the second because the grain texture is better controlled and the resin grain is more easily fixed after dusting. One advantage I see in the second is the convenience in wiping away any errors made during the painting of the sketch.

The following is a concise yet clear description by Albert Heckman of how the aquatint *Side Street* was made:

"Copper plate cleaned with a weak solution of lye;
Immersed for a few seconds in a two per cent solution of nitric acid;
Drawing with brush and india ink that had been thickened with a small amount of sugar;
Plate dried and covered immediately with liquid ground and wide brush (I make this liquid ground with twenty-five parts French turpentine, three parts wax, two parts Burgundy pitch and two parts asphalt; wax, pitch and asphalt

PLATE 26.

THE NEXT HOP by *William Heaslip*.

Original size, 14 x 11. Guide lines and base, straight etching; entire figure of mechanic and on pilot's head, liftground using a black wash suspension; on body of pilot, straight aquatint; over rest of plate, a lightly etched fine grain; resinbox and Smillie's Bath used. *(Courtesy of Kennedy & Co.)*

heated separately, then added to the turpentine and filtered);

Plate slightly heated over an open gas flame;

Washed in cold running water to lay bare the drawing;

After drying, covered with powdered resin from a silk bag;

Powder is fixed, heating slightly;

Back and edges of plate stopped-out;

Etched to a slight depth with perchloride of iron;

Whole plate washed and cleaned;

Covered again with powdered resin and heated to fixing;

Etched for a few seconds with perchloride of iron;

Sky and side of house stopped-out with varnish and also a grease crayon such as actors use for make-up; this was stippled on in many instances so as to give graduated tones with each successive stopping-out;

Five stoppings-out of other areas were made, timed by appearance of depth of bitings;

Final printing with a clean wipe, all textural effects are in the plate."

In the procedure just described the author recommends caution about heating the plate over an open gas flame during the evaporation of the liquid ground, even though turpentine has been used as the solvent. For hastening the evaporation the ordinary etching stove will do just as well. In preparing the liquid ground Margulies prefers the use of benzine to turpentine. Nankivell, as mentioned before, uses ether and ordinary etching ground. Sometimes chloroform is used if ether is not available. Naturally, the use of the last two solvents does not require any heating for evaporation to take place rapidly.

78

Chapter X

CORRECTIVE MEASURES

ANYTHING within reason can be done with a copper plate. No plate should be regarded as lost while it still retains work worth saving. Copper is a soft metal and if the artist is not averse to hard work it can be molded to his will. If I may be allowed a lapse into the facetious, a copper plate which errs can be pounded on the back and made to throw out its chest for a new lease on life. This is called *repoussage*, as every student-etcher will recognize.

Errors are usually caused by misjudging the action of the mordant. Fresh solutions, for some reason or other, often take time before getting under way; old solutions sometimes become very active. No doubt, weather conditions and the ductile state of the copper have a good deal to do with it, so that a plate is either overbitten or under-bitten.

Such errors can be prevented by testing the acid and ground by time-bitings on small pieces of copper before taking a chance with the always important plate.

The reduction of overbitten areas presents one impor-

79

tant danger: over-reduction. The slower and gentler are the manipulations of the tools employed the more certain and successful will be the outcome. The area under attack must be continuously inked and wiped after every few strokes of the burnisher, scraper, snakestone, rotten stone, emery papers, or anything else. Reducing blindly, that is, without inking, almost always results in disappointment. True, there may be a slight loss in desired texture (over-biting widens the receptacles) but, as a rule, this is not perceptible. Burnishing or scraping should be done in all directions to prevent streakiness.

Sometimes a drop of acid will give the necessary result in reducing a very small area. This is done directly on the bare copper, and can be effectively employed for getting additional tone variations when such effect was not thought of during the stopping-out and biting. Varied tonal effects can be produced by any of the reducing methods.

The correction of underbiting presents more of a problem than does overbiting. One might think that merely re-aquatinting the area with a stronger biting would solve the trouble; this is correct only when it makes no difference what kind of texture is produced. It is assumed, however, that a certain texture was sought for when the plate

PLATE 27.

TOIL OF THREE by *Arthur B. Davies*.

Original size, 6¾ x 3½. Definition, aquatint, arrived at by
stopping-out; roulette on hair and faces of upper two figures.

(Courtesy of Ferargil Galleries)

was originally grounded, and re-aquatinting will change this into something that may not be wanted.

The procedure, then, is to burnish out completely the entire underbitten area before applying a new ground. The object is to level the hills to the base of the valley, and the quickest way is to use the scraper more or less vigorously and follow that by applying various grades of emery paper, from coarse to fine, until a highly polished surface is obtained. No less efficient is the use of snakestone followed by the emery papers. This latter method may take a little longer but there is less danger of accidentally producing the drypoint line so likely to occur with the careless use of the scraper. If no machine oil is handy, the snakestone can be used with saliva, or even water. The smooth metal burnisher is too slow for thoroughly effacing an aquatint area.

In applying a ground over an already bitten area, for any reason whatsoever, it is important that a grain coarser or finer than the original be used. It may be theoretically possible for a second ground to approximate the position of the first, but the chance of getting all the granules to rest in the same place as before is remote indeed. If the attempt is made, the grain may settle in the valley leaving the hills to be leveled by the acid, the result will be a neutralization of the former aquatint, in which case the

82

PLATE 28.

THE BRIDGE by *Albert Heckman*.

Original size, 8 x 10. Neither an aquatint nor a softground but done entirely with the roulette, demonstrating the textural effect of this instrument and its possibilities as a corrective in defective aquatint (Chapter X.). *(Courtesy of Ferargil Galleries)* print will be even lighter than the underbitten reject. The rule of re-aquatinting, therefore, is to apply a grain differing in texture from that previously used.

Foul-biting occurs as a result of carelessness in stopping-out. If it is not necessary to see the etched line or mass underneath, the transparent varnish should be mixed with lampblack so that any free surface of copper can easily be detected.

The removal of a foul-bite is difficult enough in line etching, but when it occurs in aquatint it offers a serious problem. Careful scraping with the point of the scraper or burnishing with the end of the burnisher may fix it successfully, but—depending on how it looks—it may sometimes be advisable to remove the whole area and re-aquatint. Occurring in a deeply etched area it had better be left alone. Arthur B. Davies never seemed to bother much about foul-biting, but since he expressed himself with such freedom of tone, apparently these accidents do not detract from the artistic value of his work.

Always a source of annoyance is the accidental application or spreading of varnish. This may happen during the more delicate stopping-out if excess varnish has not been removed from the brush; it may happen when varnishing the edges and back of the plate. Minor accidents of this sort may temporarily be ignored until the biting is com-

PLATE 29.

REVOLT by *Alex R. Stavenitz.*

Original size, 10½ x 7. Brilliant example of aquatint worked mezzotint fashion (Chapter X.); plate irregularly grounded with dust-bag held one foot away; background stopped-out after two minutes in nitric acid 33%; rest bitten eight minutes; burnisher, scraper, etc. accomplished highlights and gradations.

(*Courtesy of Kleemann Galleries*)

pleted, when the plate is then cleaned and the small blank areas skillfully drypointed with the burr removed. Sometimes the quality of the drypoint is not desirable, in which case the roulette offers splendid possibilities for correcting white spots. There are several varieties of this instrument; the small wheel will probably render most frequent service. Firm pressure is used and the burr scraped off as with the drypoint needle.

Should accidental stopping-out be extensive it is usually best to reground the plate. One hates to do this, I know, especially when important detail work has already been done; in that case, we may continue the stopping-out so that it includes whole areas of masses of composition, bite what is left, and then apply a new ground.

Many aquatints have been made without the use of stopping-out of any sort. A plate is grounded with a fine grain and deeply bitten; from this point one proceeds as in mezzotint, working from dark into light, with any or all of the reducing implements. This method is frequently used as a corrective measure, for the purpose of adding a highlight to balance a composition or for subsequent addition of line work.

As stated in the beginning, with all these measures of correction, accidents and errors should never be thought of as the final curtain for what may turn out to be a

PLATE 30.

BREADLINE, NEW YORK by *Alex R. Stavenitz*.
Original size, 10½ x 7. Technique similar to PLATE 29.

(Courtesy of Kleemann Galleries)

splendid work of art. Careful study and planning will most always find the proper solution to what may superficially appear as a lost cause. I am of the opinion that there are very few aquatints that did not require some corrective measures before the artist considered his work satisfactorily completed.

Chapter XI

ACID-RESISTANT CRAYONS

THUS far I have carefully avoided the mention of lithographic and waxy crayons, but I believe the beginner is now sufficiently well advanced not to be confused by a presentation of further innovations in technique. It is quite likely that by this time the student-aquatinter has already developed his own particular style with perhaps a few technical innovations of his own.

It will be noticed that where there is no line of definition dividing two adjacent areas of aquatint differently bitten, there remains a sharp and sudden edge to the deeper area. If the object so bitten is a distinct entity of the composition this sharp edge no doubt is of great value for the separation of two masses of different tone, texture or perspective.

However, if this sharp separation occurs between the varying tones in the same object—other than for the purpose of depth—we get an exceedingly harsh, even crude, effect not easily corrected by the burnisher or scraper. If this should occur, for example, on a face, or body, or tree, the effect may even approach mediocrity from an artistic point of view.

No doubt many an artist has given up the medium of aquatint on account of this sharp, ugly separation which may have seemed impossible to avoid. The correction, or rather the prevention, is simple. It involves the free use of the china-marking pencil, the lithograph or wax crayon —*any fatty crayon that is resistant to acid*.

Early in the book I mentioned how fortunate it was that the resin grain made so rugged a ground, much harder and more adhesive to the copper than the ordinary hard etching ground. I had in mind its great resistance to the china-marking pencil, for by pressing firmly with the crayon on the resin ground it acts as a stopping-out wherever it is applied. By its very softness the acid-resisting material of the pencil is pressed onto the copper surface between the granules of the resin.

It is not so complete or sudden a stopping-out as varnish, but therein lies its virtue. The line it makes is wide enough to show a gradation outward from its central axis, so that were we to use it to outline a mass that had just been bitten and *dried*, immediately before the application of varnish in preparation for the next biting, the sharp edge complained of before would be eliminated.

Let us return for a moment to Test Plate II and study

PLATE 31.

FANTASIA OF THE SEA by *Frank A. Nankivell.*

Original size, 10½ x 15. Softground base with fine grain aquatint; drypoint on rocks; topping-out with varnish and crayon; some corrections with burnisher and scraper.

(Courtesy of Ferargil Galleries)

its white dividing lines; although this is not quite the best illustrative example, it will help in understanding the point I should like to make. Before any biting of the aquatint took place, I ruled these lines across the ground with the china-marking pencil. These served to protect the copper from the acid, the last line withstanding the attack for forty minutes before being partly assisted by the varnish. At the end of the biting-time for each area, the varnish was painted on with a fine brush *half way through* the dividing line of the next contiguous area, the line being thick enough to split that way. This is important, for it left the *lower half of the line* free to prevent a sharp division.

In this plate I was anxious to obtain a white line all the way through, but were I to have marked off each division separately and successively, varnishing to half way through the line at every step, I would have gotten a pleasing blend from one area to the other—painlessly, so to speak —and that might not have been suitable for this particular plate.

For emphasis, and in the interests of clarity, let me repeat the procedure. After each biting, allow the plate to dry thoroughly; define, with the acid-resisting crayon, the area that is to be varnished before placing the plate in the acid again; now stop-out this area, carrying the var-

PLATE 32.

AN OLD COURTYARD by *John Taylor Arms*.

Original size, 7½ x 6⅜. Etching and aquatint; resin-box and Dutch mordant used.   (*Courtesy of Kennedy & Co.*)

nish half way through the newly made crayon-line. When the plate is again dry, immerse it in the bath for the next biting; repeat the procedure for the next area.

With practice and man's innate ingenuity and adaptability the artist may yet evolve many further uses of the fatty crayon. In succeeding chapters I shall continue to discuss the uses of the fatty crayon in eliminating the sharp edge, in the grading of tone, in the making of a white line, and for modeling.

The old aquatinters of the last century used the lithograph crayon for lightly sketching their guide lines on the resin-grounded plate: they avoided the application of pressure because they were afraid of interfering with the action of the acid! They thereby missed the point entirely. It remained for Nankivell, as far as I know, to develop the present uses of the fatty crayon. So extensively is this crayon used by Nankivell that he has come to regard it as of equal, if not superior, importance to the stopping-out varnish. I almost believe he could dispense with the varnish entirely and be free to display his skill with his sharp pointed, flat edged, thin or thick, multicolored china-marking pencils.

Chapter XII

THE WHITE LINE

GORDON GRANT was present at one of Nankivell's demonstrations before some of his pupils. Grant was requested to draw a sketch with the china-marking pencil on a small resin-grounded plate; he was told to bear in mind that he would be making highlights (which would vary with the pressure he used). The plate was bitten for two minutes in the hydrochloric acid bath and "struck off." In this state it could have stood alone as an effective white line sketch on a gray background, but for the sake of the demonstration, Grant continued with drypoint for shade and definition. The result was a fine composition of black, gray and white.

To produce white lines in this way the point of the pencil must be sharpened after every few strokes, because firm pressure is necessary for it to sink in between the granules onto the copper surface and this, of course, dulls the soft point very quickly. The line it makes is not absolutely clean-cut, but because it isn't it can be

95

employed for certain soft effects not possible with other white lines.

The usual method of getting a white line is to apply the stopping-out varnish with a very fine brush. Owing to the tendency of the varnish to spread many a plate has to be regrounded before this delicate procedure is successful. I have never seen a complete white line sketch on a black background done this way; one can easily imagine the disappointment of the artist who would try to use stopping-out varnish for anything beyond making the customary lightning streak, the glint on a pupil, a distant lamplight, a reflection, or some such other single application. I have seen, however, the print of a line etched plate whose surface was carefully inked with a roller so that none of the ink found its way into the lines; the result was a white line sketch on a black background—but this is not aquatint.

Sometimes it is possible carefully to burnish out a white line, usually thick, of course; its whiteness, however, is likely to be questionable. Such a line serves best as definition; as definition it can be quite successful.

After a great deal of experimentation for the purpose of getting a clean-cut white line in aquatint, I finally hit upon so simple and direct a method that on its first trial I felt rather foolish for having looked for something more

complicated. Briefly, the stopping-out is done before the ground is applied!

The procedure is as follows: Dip an ordinary pen into the stopping-out varnish, wipe the excess off on the neck of the bottle or rim of the container, and *slowly* draw on the clean surface of the copper wherever the line or sketch is to be, keeping the hands off the plate. For the white horizontal lines in Test Plate I I used a stub pen, but much finer lines are possible with a fine pen-point. Should the varnish run at any place, one merely has to wipe it off with a piece of cloth or cotton wet with alcohol, wait for evaporation, and try again. When the line or sketch is completed the varnish is allowed to dry. If the plate has been touched anywhere, carefully clean it with a cloth dampened in benzine without disturbing the varnish-lines. The plate is now resin-grounded in the usual way; the momentary heating of the plate for the grain fixation will not affect the varnish. Incidentally, I may add, I used a French lacquer varnish in Test Plate I; it seems to dry quickly and firmly. I claim no originality for my procedure—it's far too simple.

PLATE 34.

FORTUNE by *Frank A. Nankivell.*
Original size, 10 x 8. Complete sketch with an acid-resistant crayon producing a white line on a black background (Chapter XII.).

(Courtesy of Ferargil Galleries)

GRADATED AQUATINT

WHEN well done, the graded aquatint is a fine technical and artistic expression. Not only does it give contour to an object, but, when it is applied over the plate as a whole, it serves to direct the eye toward the point of interest and acts as a stimulant to the imagination.

A true plastic process is the mezzotint-like method of burnishing an aquatint described in the last chapter. Grading this way requires constant vigilance lest too much be done; that, of course, would ruin the effect. Pressure is applied firmly where one wants the extreme highlight and at each stroke towards the dark the instrument is swept upward off the plate. Great care must be exercised if the scraper is used, and the plate should be inked and wiped often. The feeling of the artist must be transmitted to and interpreted by the instrument; with patience success is literally around the corner. If gradation is to be accomplished this way one should have it in mind while the plate lies in the acid; overbiting can then be inten-

PLATE 35.

FROM AN OFFICE WINDOW by *C. R. W. Nevinson.*

Original size, 10 x 7. Pure aquatint; graded biting, partly burnishing.

(Courtesy of Frederick Keppel & Co.)

tionally produced, and a good field for the operation will thus be offered.

When a single area is involved, such as a sky, dipping the plate is the easiest and surest way of getting a graduated tone. Everything else should be varnished out before proceeding. Decide upon the biting-time of the darkest portion and place that in the bath first. Then with an eye on the clock tilt the plate slowly further into the tray, regulating the movement so that the entire biting-time will be taken up just as the area which should remain lightest is reached. If the time required is too long to do this effectively in one dip, then the maneuver is repeated several times; the plate is rinsed thoroughly and quickly in water after each dip.

In gradating several masses of the composition with the dip method, the plate should be grounded separately for each mass—unless it is convenient to handle two areas at a time, or, if they are wide apart, successively after each finished area is stopped-out. Separate grounding affords an excellent opportunity for the use of different textures. I should suggest that the foreground remain coarse in texture, and that as the distance is approached the texture be allowed to get finer (and lighter in tone) gradually. This is similar to the artistic convention used in line etch-

PLATE 36.

OBOE by *Harry Sternberg*.

    Original size, 10¾ x 6⅞. Line etching base and defi-
nition; graded aquatint directing the eye to central
figure.   *(Courtesy of Weyhe Gallery)*

ing, where foreground lines are deep and wide apart, distant lines close and lightly bitten.

The "spit" method frequently employed in line etching does not result in so even a gradation, but it gives more interesting effects because of the possibilities of obtaining varied qualities of tone. The area to be attacked is first moistened with saliva and the acid applied with a brush, first on the portion which is to be darkest; one works gradually towards the highlight. One may also apply the acid with an eye-dropper, but some sort of a brush should be used for the painting. The acid should be frequently blotted up with ordinary blotting paper before the mordant acts too strongly on what eventually is to be the highlight. This maneuver is repeated until the desired effect is reached.

The use of acid-resistant crayons to make graduating tones has already been mentioned. This requires careful penciling from light into dark, allowing for eventual penetrations by the acid. William Heaslip's *Airport* is a fine example; it shows the gradation of the floodlights obtained in this manner.

Graded texture is also possible but is not so easily executed. One may follow the method I have just described (coarse texture for foreground and fine texture for distance) but as each individual mass retains its own texture

PLATE 37.

IN WHARFDALE by *Percival Gaskell.*

Original size, 9¼ x 7¾. Weak biting for distance, deep biting for foreground
(Chapter XIII.). *(Courtesy of Schwartz Galleries)*

throughout, this is really gradating by suggestion. With skillful use of the sieve, coarse grains may be applied in any direction and in increasing amounts as one nears the edge of the plate. Here again is an artistic expression which will depend entirely upon the artist's personal feeling. I mention it merely to show that anything can be done with the fascinating medium of aquatint.

Chapter XIV

SCHEMATA

ENORMOUS freedom of action lies with the artist. He has nothing more to guide him than a mental image of what should eventually appear on the plate. To compose as one goes along, with imagination holding full sway and without following any sort of plan has sometimes yielded fine artistic results. Once the artist commands full control of technique, technique is rendered secondary in importance to his expression. Such is the case in all fine works of art, plan or no plan.

Not all of us, however, are gifted with such spontaneity. Most artists would much prefer having at least an outline of an original sketch to serve as a guide, and to plan the procedure carefully. At any rate, if one is to reproduce a specific composition in facsimile, it is quite important to draw up a detailed plan of action to minimize the possibility of overlooking an important highlight or shadow. One does forget to allow the acid to bite only two minutes on this spot and four minutes on that spot, and to aquatint for a coarse grain here and re-aquatint for a gradation

107

there; and, before one realizes it, this area is stopped-out when it should have been bitten and that area is bitten when it should have been stopped-out.

In the plate *Airport*, William Heaslip first carefully etched in with softground the hangar, figures, and other structural objects and parts of the sky. He followed a mental plan, with the original sketch in front of him. The structural objects were bolstered up for detail and solidity by line etching through the hard etching ground. Then followed a gradated bite (dip method) on the sky, with a fine grain resin-aquatint, all lights (landing lights, beacon lights and floodlights) graded with the acid-resistant crayon. A trial proof showed all objects too sharply defined, disjointed, and not quite in shadow; another resin ground was laid, extreme highlights varnished out, the crayon again brought into play, and the balance "tied" together with a two-minute bite. Smillie's Bath was used throughout. Then came another trial proof followed by the usual finishing touches with burnisher, emery papers, roulette, etc. The entire procedure of five main steps took about twenty hours over a period of three weeks. The three weeks, of course, has nothing to do with it—it might just as well have been twenty hours in one stretch. I mention it only to show that inspiration has no

PLATE 38.

AIRPORT by *William Heaslip*.
Original size, 12 x 15. Described in Chapter XIV.

(Courtesy of Kennedy & Co.)

time limit, for it certainly required inspiration to produce this masterpiece in spite of all interruptions.

Quite upsetting my own personal prejudice against the use of strong mordants, Earl Horter made his fine aquatint, *The Kitchen*, not only with the fifty per cent nitric I advise against, but with the pure undiluted acid. It proves—anything or nothing! However, Horter describes his scheme of action as follows:

"One resin ground laid on by shaking out of a bag, stopping-out the whites with orange shellac in which is mixed enough lampblack to see it easily on the plate; then immersed in fifty per cent nitric for every light tone.... I make brushes out of wrapping paper folded into quarter inch strips; I use several of these because the acid destroys them. I then pour pure nitric in a small saucer and a regular solution of fifty per cent in another, and water in a glass, with blotters near by. I then practically make a watercolor with the acid—pouring on the strong acid for intensive parts and stopping out here and there as parts get finished, watching carefully through glass or testing with my fingernail parts which I can afford to lose. I use a blotter to regulate passages, etc., occasionally cleaning the plate under spigot, and tapping with chamois. There is of course a little more than this but I just can't put it into words."

PLATE 39.

.THE KITCHEN by *Earl Horter*.
Original size, 12⅜ x 10⅜. Described in Chapter XIV.

(*Courtesy of Grand Central Art Galleries*)

Earl Horter put it into words very well, especially where he mentions the procedure as being practically that of making a watercolor. In his letter he further describes his technique:

"Sometimes on a plate I use two or three different degrees of resin, coarse to fine. Sometimes I lay a fine ground in a particular place and bite it lightly, then use a coarse ground over it after cleaning off the plate. I never use a dust box nor resort to just successive bitings. I manipulate every plate and use the utmost care, but I depend on accidentals for interest and never know exactly how it is turning out. I use copper exclusively, and trace the drawing on the plate with the use of carbon paper."

Alexander Z. Kruse, however, traces his drawing on the grounded plate by chalking the back of the paper containing the sketch or outline and lightly going over the lines with a pencil; the chalk-lines are easily blown off and do not interfere with the action of the acid. This artist has more or less a fixed routine of procedure which he uses for most of his plates. He divides the range of highlights to blacks (as in the pure aquatint, *Sky Gazers*) into six stages; he uses Smillie's Bath. His procedure is as follows:

Extreme highlight, stopped-out, no biting;
Toned highlight, two minutes of biting;
Light gray, five minutes (three more minutes of biting);

PLATE 40.

SKY GAZERS by *Alexander Z. Kruse*
   Original size, 9 x 12. Described in Chapter XIV.   (*Courtesy of Weyhe Gallery*)

Dark gray, ten minutes (five more minutes of biting);
Light black, thirty minutes (twenty more minutes of biting);
Deep black, forty-five minutes (thirty minutes more of biting).

This biting-time, it will be noticed, is somewhat similar to those followed in our test plates. Kruse employs a fine grain coating from a resin box.

For the making of the very beautiful print *Upper Mill, Great Valley*, S. Gordon Smyth used the following procedure which he describes in his own words.

"My method of getting a result is tedious and rather strenuous, and, because of blind handling, requires supreme care. Needless to say, the finished product is never just what is hoped for. On the other hand, in the development of a plate one frequently finds something that was not expected—qualities, even through mistakes, that add rather than detract. One learns what to do and what not to do and applies his gained knowledge to subsequent work.

"My preliminary studies are made in either watercolor or pastel. I make a very elaborate drawing with a lithograph crayon on cameo paper. In this drawing I work out the minutest detail, and, while so doing, anticipate my procedure with the acid. This drawing is transferred in outline on tracing paper and retraced upon the grounded plate with carbon paper. Before this is done, however, I

had already etched into the copper most of the outline to serve as the more important guides for the stopping-out.

"Fifty per cent nitric acid is used, and I always make a key plate of a few square inches to let me know how the acid is working. The plate is grounded by means of a silk bag containing the resin powder.

"I usually place the plate in the bath about six times in the following graduated scale: fifteen seconds in order to dull the gloss of the plate, thirty seconds, seventy-five seconds, two and three-quarters minutes, six minutes, and finally for an indefinite short period for deep blacks, constantly watching the plate for any possibility of the ground breaking. If this happens on a large area the plate is probably destroyed; otherwise, for a small area, stippling with a fine point will correct the accident.

"Between each bath I manipulate my masses, large and small, with diluted acid, treating it as a watercolor, and stopping-out accordingly. In place of a brush I roll up a piece of heavy wrapping paper using one end for acid and the other for pure water. In this way I get interesting variations.

"This procedure is used in the case of one grounding. A plate may require several different groundings. In one of my plates I re-aquatinted ten times using the foregoing method on each occasion."

The standard procedure was followed by C. Jac Young in the application of the tonal effects supporting the straight line etching, *Symphonic Poem*. He took the following steps:

1. Complete composition, except for sky, etched in the usual manner with nitric acid fifty per cent. This might have stood alone as entirely complete if tones left by the ink during the printing could easily be repeated, but the artist decided it was much simpler to employ a clean wipe throughout the edition and at the same time obtain a pleasing texture.

2. Plate cleaned and placed in resin-box twice for one minute each.

3. After fixing and cooling, parts of snow, water, tree and stumps, and sides of first two houses stopped-out.

4. The whole placed in nitric acid twenty-five per cent for ten seconds; rinsed and dried.

5. All of foreground snow, roofs and sides of last house stopped-out.

6. Plate placed in bath for ten more seconds; rinsed and dried.

7. Distant snow mounds and parts of water stopped-out.

8. Lower half of plate, holding the water of the sketch,

immersed in bath for one minute; rinsed and dried.

9. Water stopped-out.

10. Graded bite in sky, dip method (see Chapter XIII),
making a total time in the acid of approximately two
minutes for darkest area graded towards a highlight
of seventy seconds. Then rinsed and dried.

Chapter XV

AQUATINTING FOR COLOR

THE decided increase in the number of exhibitions of color prints within the last few years shows the growing interest in this branch of the arts. Compared to color etching, the making of a colored woodcut or a colored lithograph is relatively easy. This should be sufficient to challenge the proud aquatinter to a test of his genius.

An aquatint printed with colored pigment—not a black-and-white print colored by means of brush or spray—is akin to, and can be just as beautiful as, a painting on canvas. On the other hand, it can be so poorly executed that it will be worse than no color at all. Many factors strongly influence the result; one should at least possess a good color sense.

Admitting my own deficiencies in the finer appreciation of color values and in the practical side of the technique of color printing, I should have preferred to eliminate this chapter entirely were it not so essentially a part of the subject of aquatint. Again, therefore, I consider myself fortunate in the generous assistance of Nankivell.

This artist assures me that the subject is far too extensive to include in one short chapter. He suggests that I merely present the cardinal points and refer the reader to the textbooks on color printing and to the always interesting field of personal experimentation.

Simply put, aquatinting for color is a matter of correct tone, texture and depth for each particular pigment used. In other words, one must know before etching the plate what the final color effects are to be; otherwise, the artist places himself in the position of being dictated to by his own plate! The quality and color of the pigments on hand, or the lack of any of these, should never be allowed to dictate the printing. The best of material must be used and the proper blending and consistency of ink made, else too many prints will have to be rejected and the artist will be discouraged from further employment of this medium.

As mentioned before, certain color effects require certain textures of grain and certain depths of biting. For example, if a dark red color is wanted the area must be deeply bitten with a fine grain; a lightly bitten area or too coarse a texture may print pink. The same relationship applies to orange and light orange, brown and tan, etc. Biting must be continued further than is required by a black-and-white print, and, in general, a fine grain tex-

PLATE 42.

THE FLIGHT by *R. Ward Binks.*
Original size, 7½ x 11. Sharply defined flat tints supporting lightly etched guide lines; made for color yet printing effectively as a black-and-white (Chapter XV.).

(Courtesy of Harlow, McDonald & Co.)

ture employed where intense colors are desired. Of course, one can mix his colors to approximate an effect regardless of the intrinsic tone and texture of the aquatint, but this may result in a loss of depth and brilliancy—that certain richness of color that often spells the word *masterpiece*.

It follows that many plates aquatinted for color make weird black-and-white impressions. One must bear this point in mind when etching the plate: if black-and-whites are required the plate should be etched accordingly and the edition printed before re-aquatinting for color.

It is not my intention to make the subject appear too difficult. Actually, many completely aquatinted plates are good both for black-and-whites and for color. Sometimes only ocasional areas need be changed; that, of course, is easily done. The black-and-white aquatint, if artistically executed for correct values, is strongly suggestive of color by virtue of its tones and textures, so that red lips will print black, pink cheeks light gray, brown hair dark gray, etc. These areas will very likely take their respective pigments without further aquatinting.

In printing a coarse-textured aquatint with color, tones left by the ink on the surface area may give the desired effect. This, naturally, more or less eliminates the grain texture, and streakiness is likely to manifest itself.

Colored ink left on a non-aquatinted area often gives

PLATE 43.

HERTZLER'S MILL by *S. Gordon Smyth.*
Original size, 9¾ x 15. Same technique as PLATE 41.

a smudgy appearance, if it adheres at all; it is better to wipe the plate clean and pull the impression on colored paper. Although not exactly a color etching as we understand it, printing this way can be very effective and suggestive if the proper combination of ink and paper is used for the particular subject of the composition.

There are two general methods of printing an aquatint in color. One is the *single impression,* which is the method Nankivell chooses. First he applies a neutral color over the whole plate and wipes it dry; then, with separate dabber for each, the different colors are put on their respective places successively, after wiping—or at once and then wiped carefully over the cold plate so that blending is kept at a minimum. The plate is then warmed and is ready for the imprint.

The other method is by *superimposed impressions.* This can be employed in either of two ways. The first—probably the more frequently used—involves the use of only the original plate on which the colors are applied and printed separately and consecutively on the same paper. The second method, called the *multiple plate method,* uses a separate plate for each color, usually about four plates including the original. In either case, the method of superimposed impressions requires more time than does the single impression; each pigment must be thoroughly dry before the next one can be applied. Meantime the paper has to be dampened before each impress; this expands it—and perhaps slightly distorts the outline of the printing already on the paper—sufficiently to render exact superimposition difficult. Here, as in everything else, practice makes perfect.

Chapter XVI

RESURRECTED INSPIRATIONS

MANY a rejected line etching or drypoint has ultimately been changed into a fine aquatint, proof that a plate should seldom be regarded as entirely lost. Granted that the artist originally thought of his subject matter in terms of line, and that a foul-bite or some other error spoiled what might have been an excellent work of art, *but*:

Did the artist make a new plate of the same subject? Did the second plate show the same spontaneity and freedom of expression as the first? Was his determination held by the force of inspiration, or did his disgust relegate the original idea to the scrap-heap of disappointment?

There must be in every etcher's studio a few plates standing up against the wall in some remote corner, oxidized and dusty, mute evidence of dormant or suppressed inspiration. Incidentally, if they are really so badly gone that they are utterly beyond rescue, the backs of these plates offer a most interesting medium quite suitable

126

PLATE 44.

STRAWBERRIES by *Wuanita Smith*.

Original size, 8 x 10. Coarse grain, dust-bag; fifty per cent nitric acid bath for one, two and three minutes, followed by the pure acid applied with feather for deep blacks.

(Courtesy of Grant Gallery)

for aquatint. In fact, Arthur B. Davies preferred to use the back of a plate rather than its polished surface.

The etcher must now turn his thoughts to masses and textures and tones, carefully studying the possibilities of converting a line drawing into a painting. The old plate is cleaned with soap, water and stiff brush followed by vinegar and salt; the burr, if any, is removed—drypoint can be added again later if necessary—and overbitten lines subjected to repoussage; foul-biting is reduced to a minimum by the scraper, burnisher and emery papers, and the whole plate polished as best one can.

A clean print is taken of what now is left on the plate and this is studied from the painter's angle. Watercolor, or wash, or crayon is applied to the print, retaining some of the definition here, covering some of the definition there, effacing foul-biting with deep tones—anything at all to build up a composition which will effectively tell its story. At this point it should be easy for the artist to determine whether he now possesses a work of art worth reproducing on copper as an aquatint.

Should you run across a horrified purist who tells you that media should not be mixed, humor him if you will, but, insist that it is the beauty of the final print that counts and not so much the many methods used in its production.

Mixed methods should be blended so harmoniously

PLATE 45.

CONSTRUCTION by *Harry Sternberg*.

Original size, Diameter, 10⅛. Line etching base and fine grain aquatint; some modeling on figure with burnisher.   (*Courtesy of Macbeth Galleries*)

that their individual detection can be ascertained only on close scrutiny or with the aid of a magnifying glass—if at all.

Another cause for stimulated confidence and a source for renewed inspiration that comes with a thorough knowledge of aquatint is the ability to reproduce on copper, in facsimile if desired, one's best watercolors and wash-drawings. Most of the great aquatinters of the past and present have done this without having detracted in any way from the monetary value of their original. This is a fact—forgive my plebeianism—which should never be completely disregarded by any artist. Indeed, it must be a source of great satisfaction to possess not only a print of the plate that reproduced it but the original work of art itself, a most desirable combination for any collection.

POSTSCRIPT AND BIBLIOGRAPHY

It is my hope that some day this book will be revised to include new processes of aquatint that the artist's inventiveness may develop. I have tried to make this practical treatise as complete as possible, but there must be interesting phases of technique in use today that thus far have not come to my knowledge. Any information that will materially contribute to the advancement of the art of aquatint will receive careful laboratory analysis and will be incorporated in future revisions.

A good deal has been written about the history and appreciation of the subject, not only in book form but also in numerous articles. Most of these can be found, amply catalogued, in the more important libraries such as The New York Public Library and The British Museum. One such article, written by Frank Weitenkampf, refers succinctly to aquatint as "an art much used but seldom discussed."

Quite an elaborate book on its history, and a fine one to own for one's library, is *Aquatint Engraving* by S. T.

Prideaux, published by Duckworth & Co., London, 1909; it includes brief descriptions of technique.

A good step-by-step description of the author's method of printing in color, with two fine examples reproduced and described, can be found in *Color Etching: A Practical Treatise* by Hugh Paton, published by Simpkin, Marshall, Hamilton, Kent & Co., Ltd., London, 1909.

One must not, of course, leave out that complete textbook by E. S. Lumsden, *The Art of Etching*; it contains good descriptions of the aquatint processes, including some very fine reproductions of representative examples with accompanying technical descriptions by their respective artists. It is published by J. B. Lippincott Company of Philadelphia.

Among the more recent publications, some good points on the subjects of both softground and aquatint can be obtained from *Practical Engraving and Etching* by E. G. Lutz, published by Charles Scribner's Sons of New York and London.

John Taylor Arms' *Handbook of Print Making and Print Makers,* published by the Macmillan Company, New York, 1934, contains brief descriptions of the technique and concise histories of every branch of print making, including aquatint. The book is superbly written and should be on the shelves of any library.

Postscript and Bibliography

In *The Etcher's Handbook* written by P. G. Hamerton and published in 1881 by Charles Roberson & Co., London, can be found some interesting methods of etching which are not frequently used, but which may serve as guides for future development.

There are other books, some very ancient and out of print, in which the interested reader will no doubt find great pleasure. I highly recommend such reading to the student-aquatinter and to the art lover in general; for a knowledge of the history of the subject is unquestionably essential to a keener appreciation of the various ramifications of this fascinating medium of beauty.

Glossary

In view of the fact that the etcher's vocabulary may be unfamiliar to many art lovers and art students, I am appending definitions of those terms for which adequate explanation cannot be found in the dictionary:

AQUATINT—a method of engraving a metal plate, usually of copper, by means of certain types of mordants and certain types of grain so that it will print tonal and textural masses. This, as described in Chapters III and VIII, is done in either of two main ways: one, by fixing onto the plate surface an acid-resistant powder or grain (such as resin, asphaltum, etc.) around which the acid attacks the free metal, or, two, by breaking up in a granular manner an already fixed acid-resistant covering of the plate with salt or sand, in which case the acid attacks the exposed metal where these granules had rested. Another method described involves the use of a powder (sulphur) which acts as its own mordant (corrosive) when applied in a certain manner (Chapter VIII).

"BATTERY EFFECT"—a phenomenon whereby differences of potential in various parts of the plate, partly due to impurities of the copper, cause an increase in chemical activity over and above the normal action of an acid on metal; this may result, in the case of aquatint, in irregular biting.

BITE—the action of the mordant on the copper; to etch or etch into, a term derived from the Dutch meaning "to eat."

BITING-TIME—the length of time a plate or part of a plate has been exposed to the action of a mordant.

"BOLSTER"—to *support* an already—but insufficiently—engraved area with additional work, by means of the same or any other medium, for the purpose of increasing solidity.

CLEAN WIPE—often referred to as a "hard wipe," when, during the process of printing an engraving, the ink is entirely wiped off the free surface of the plate and left only in or on the engraved lines or grain; the subsequent print, therefore, clearly shows the work that has been done by the acid or instrument employed.

CROSS-HATCHED—closely drawn lines criss-crossing each other in any direction or directions.

DEFINITION—outline, either to enclose or separate masses.

"DRAWING UP"—the molecular attraction of an applied emulsion or suspension on a smooth surface; "buckling," used similarly in the text, is the separation of the emulsion from the smooth copper surface owing to the lack of sufficient adhesiveness.

DUST-BAG—a bag, usually silk, containing powder, usually resin.

DUSTING—the application of any type of grain onto a copper plate from a dust-box, dust-bag, sieve or by hand-sprinkling for the purpose of making an aquatint.

DRYPOINT—a branch of the engraving art, often classified under the generic term of *etching,* wherein no acid is employed but lines or dots are dug or scratched into the surface of a copper plate, in the making of a sketch, by means of a sharp, steel needle or by an instrument possessing a cutting edge such as a knife; since no copper is eaten away, as with a true etching, that metal dug out in the formation of the groove is thrown up on either side or both sides of the line, depending on how the instrument was held, like the formation of breastworks in the making of a trench; this breastwork is called the "burr," owing to its irregular and corrugated appearance. The process of drypoint, therefore, is the interesting combination of intaglio and relief, and since the burr holds as much ink as the line it came from the resulting print has a furry, characteristic appearance.

ENGRAVING—in its generic sense, a term employed to include all processes of metal plate reproduction; used in a specific sense it refers to those processes that do not involve the use of acid, particularly *line engraving* wherein lines are produced by an instrument called a *burin,* and *stipple engraving* where dots are employed for the production of tones and textures and made with a sharp needle; in both these latter processes the burr is removed leaving the methods entirely intaglio.

ETCHING—in a generic sense, a term employed to include not only those processes of engraving which involve the use of a mordant but often drypoint; in its specific sense, it refers to that process where lines are bitten into a copper plate which was first covered with an acid-resistant material called a *ground* through which a sketch was drawn with a sharp needle.

ETCHING GROUND—any acid-resistant material used to cover a metal plate for the purpose of making an etching; the material consists of various combinations of wax, resin, asphaltum, pitch, mastic, and other gums of similar type.

ETCHING STOVE—a stove having a solid, flat top, usually about two feet long and one foot wide, and heated by gas at only one end to permit of a graded temperature.

FATTY RAG—an inky rag, one that has already been used in wiping a plate; the purpose of its subsequent use is to prevent a sudden removal of ink in the initial wiping of a plate.

FEATHERED—the use of an ordinary feather, or a cotton swab, or a brush made of paper, for the purpose of removing the bubbles produced by the action of an ebullient acid on the copper plate.

FOUL-BITE—the accidental biting of the acid where it was not wanted.

LITHOGRAPHY—a process of print making wherein a sketch is made with a grease crayon on stone—sometimes on zinc or aluminum—which is then treated by a weak acid and a solution of gum; the principle involved is the antipathy of grease and water so that when ink is applied it adheres only to the sketch, and the print therefrom has the same texture as the stone surface and the crayon used.

MEDIUM—a method of expression such as drypoint, softground etching, engraving, and so forth.

MEZZOTINT—a process of engraving wherein a flat instrument, called a *rocker,* having a toothed, convex edge and a convenient handle, is made to rock over a copper plate evenly in every direction until a desired area is completely broken up into a solid mass of burr which, when inked, prints an intense velvety black; from this point, a sketch, with its highlights and gradations, is burnished and scraped out by more or less leveling off the burr.

MORDANT—any corroding substance used in etching.

PULL—action of turning the etching press and making an impression.

REPOUSSAGE—the process of hammering the back of a plate to reduce or eliminate an overbitten area in front by literally pushing it up to the level of the surface area.

RETROUSSAGE—the process of dragging some of the ink out of lines or receptacles onto the surface area during the wiping of a plate for the purpose of changing the appearance of the original texture.

ROULETTE—an instrument having a toothed wheel the object of which is to produce easily a series of dots, giving an effect similar to stipple engraving; it is sometimes used over the grounded plate which is then etched, but more often it is employed directly over the bare copper and the resulting burr may or may not be removed.

STEELFACING—an electrolytic process whereby a thin coating of steel is "fused" on the face of a copper plate for the purpose of preventing the sketch from wearing down too soon during the printing of a large edition.

STOPPING-OUT—the process of varnishing an area of the plate to prevent that part from being attacked by the acid.

STRAIGHT AQUATINT—aquatint made according to the standard method of procedure as described in Chapter III; also used to imply "pure" aquatint.

STRAIGHT GROUND—ordinary hard etching ground; in Chapter IX the term refers to the precipitated hard etching ground after the ether had evaporated.

STRAIGHT LINE—referred to etching, pure line etching.

STRUCK OFF—printed.

WASH DRAWING—drawing in watercolor, usually black, using flat tints of very little texture.

WHITE SPOTS—white as they appear on the print; they are caused by large resin granules falling on the plate during the dusting of it, or by accidental drops of varnish during the stopping-out.